easy piano

the fray how to save a life

ISBN: 978-1-4234-3412-2

HAL•LEONARD®
CORPORATION
7777 W. BLUEMOUND RD. P.O. BOX 13819 MILWAUKEE, WI 53213

In Australia Contact:
Hal Leonard Australia Pty. Ltd.
4 Lentara Court
Cheltenham, Victoria, 3192 Australia
Email: ausadmin@halleonard.com.au

Visit Hal Leonard Online at
www.halleonard.com

SHE IS

Words and Music by JOSEPH KING
and ISAAC SLADE

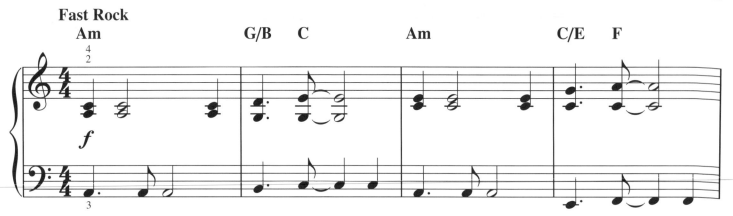

Do not get me___ wrong,___
It's all up in the air___

___ I can - not wait for you___ to come home.___
___ and we___ stand still to see___ what comes down.___

For now, you're not here___ and I'm___ not there. It's like___ we're
I don't know where it is, I don't___ know when, but I____ want

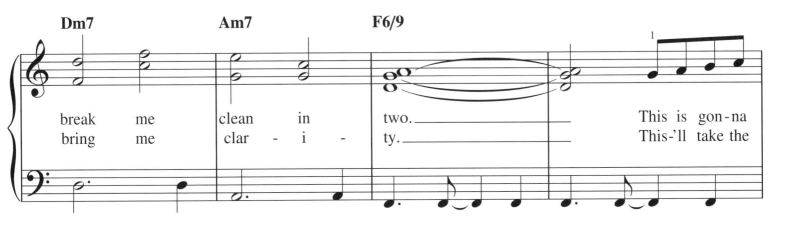

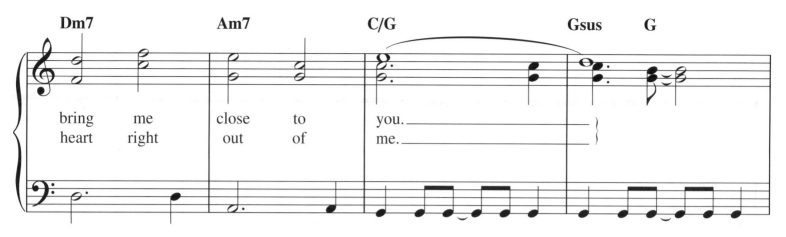

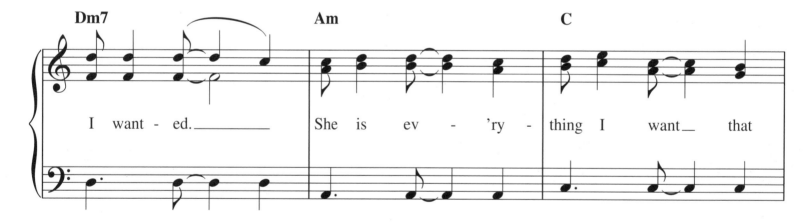

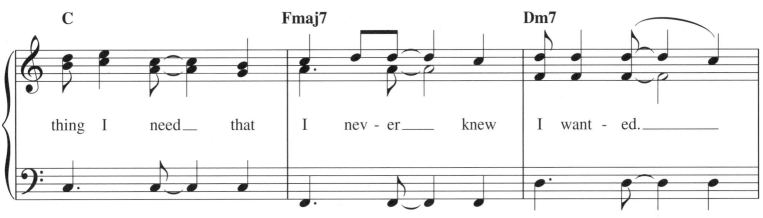

thing I need___ that | I nev - er___ knew | I want - ed.___

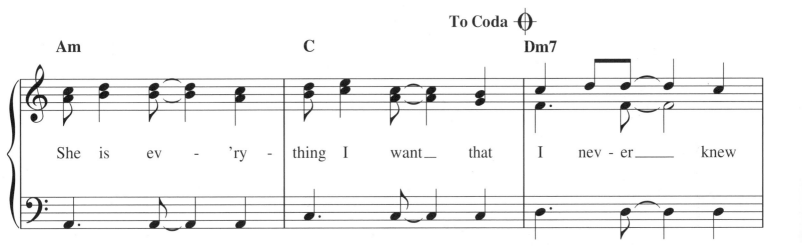

She is ev - 'ry - thing I want___ that | I nev - er___ knew

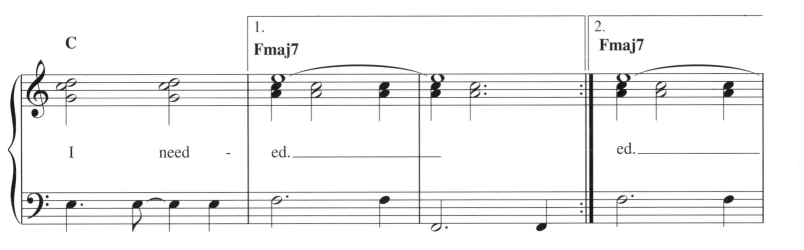

I need - ed.___ | ed.___

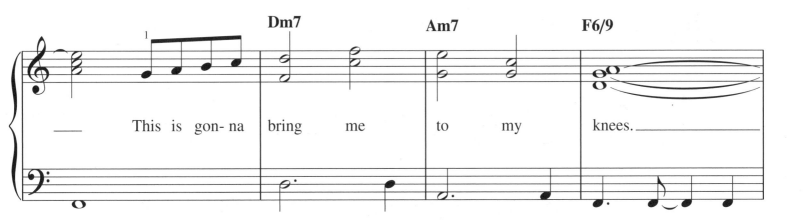

___ This is gon- na bring me to my knees.___

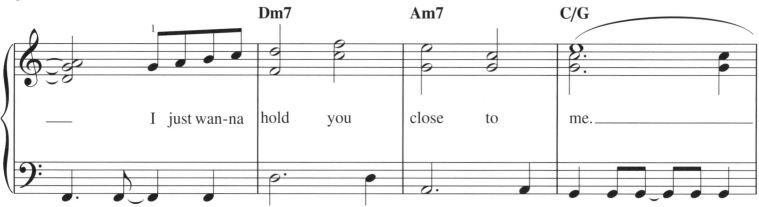

I just wan-na hold you close to me. ___

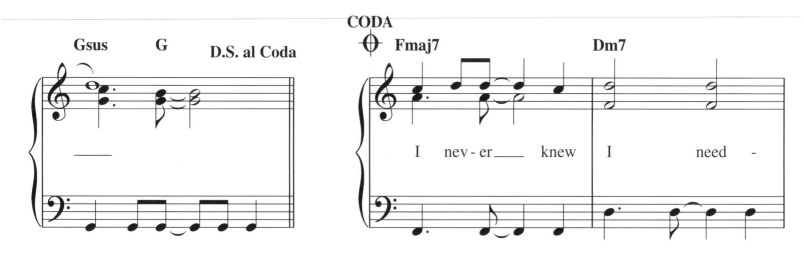

I nev-er ___ knew I need-

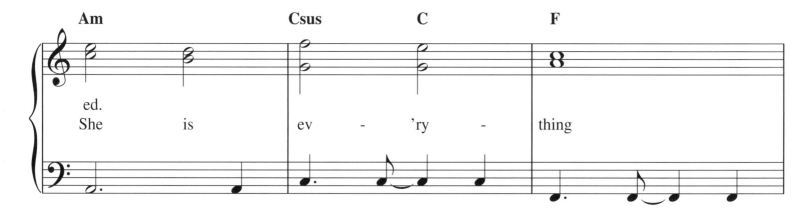

ed.
She is ev-'ry- thing

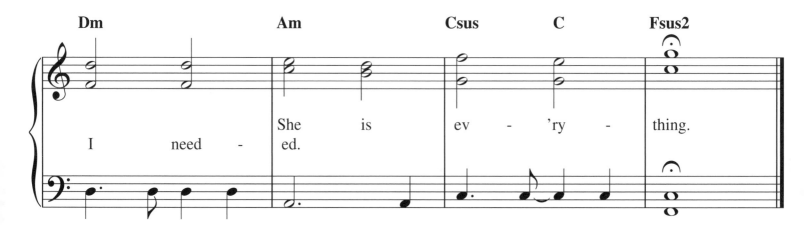

I need- ed. She is ev-'ry- thing.

OVER MY HEAD
(Cable Car)

Words and Music by JOSEPH KING
and ISAAC SLADE

Moderately fast

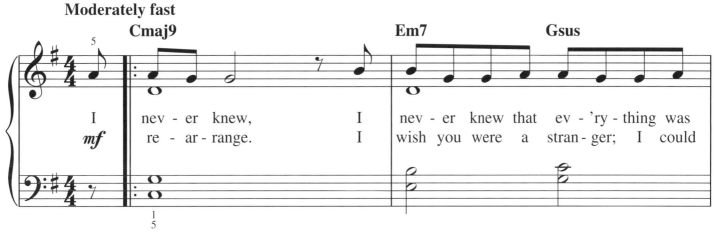

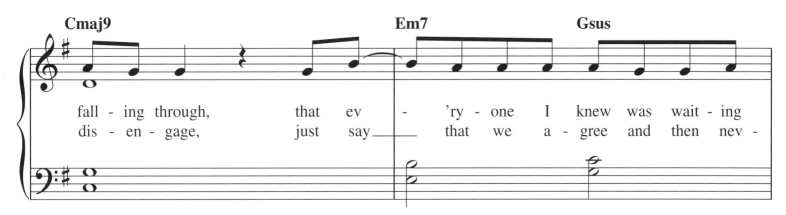

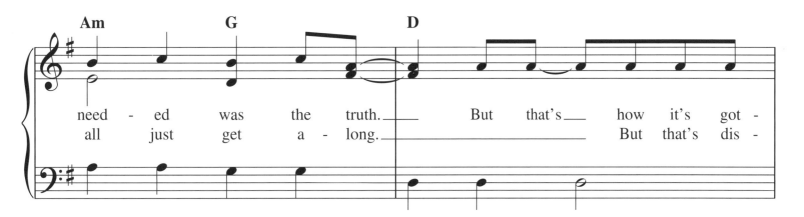

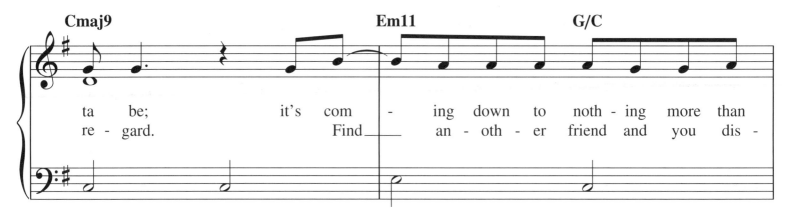

ta be; it's com - ing down to noth - ing more than
re - gard. Find___ an - oth - er friend and you dis -

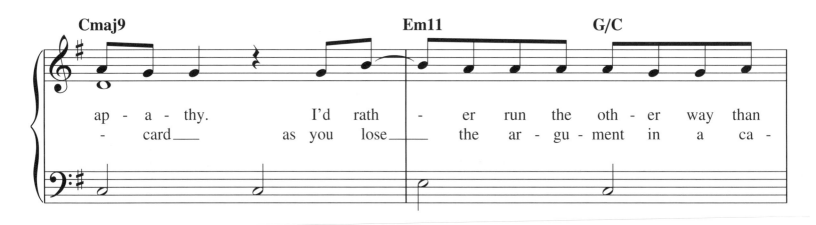

ap - a - thy. I'd rath - er run the oth - er way than
- card___ as you lose___ the ar - gu - ment in a ca -

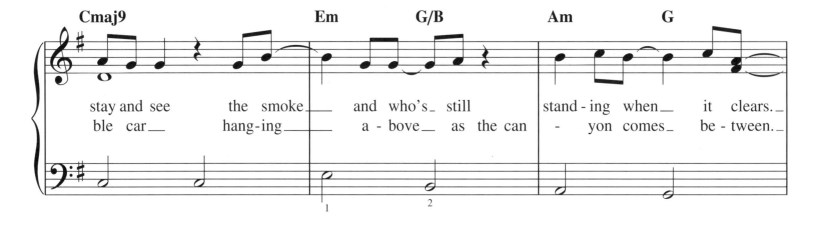

stay and see the smoke___ and who's_ still stand - ing when_ it clears._
ble car_ hang - ing___ a - bove_ as the can - yon comes_ be - tween._

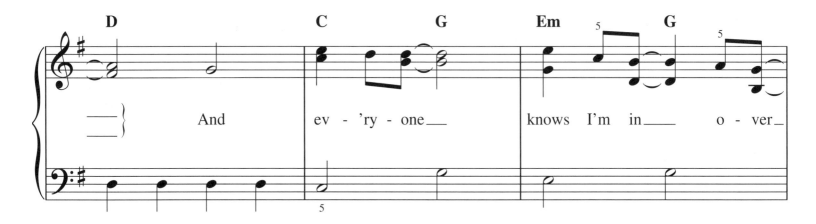

___ } And ev - 'ry - one___ knows I'm in___ o - ver_

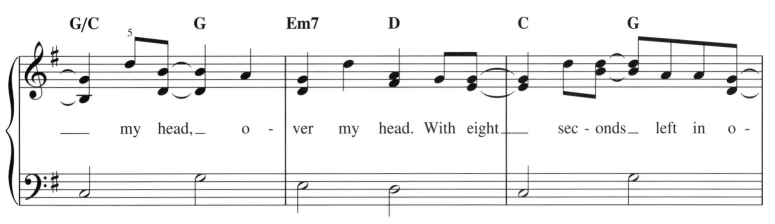

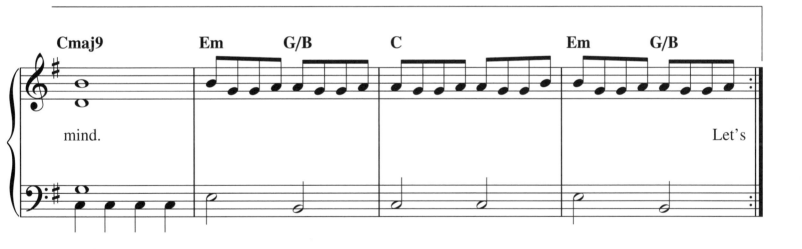

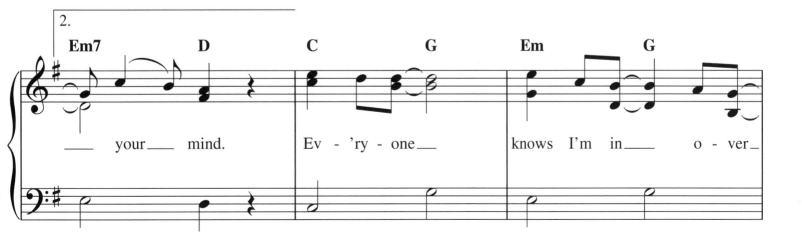

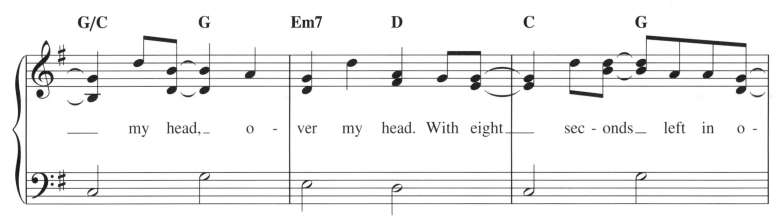

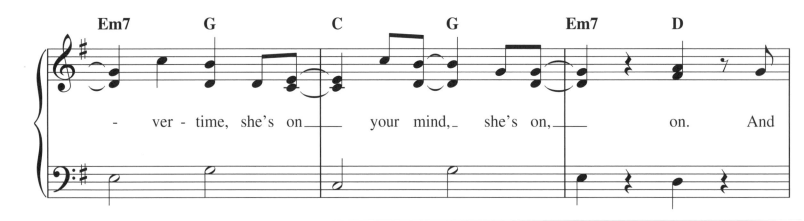

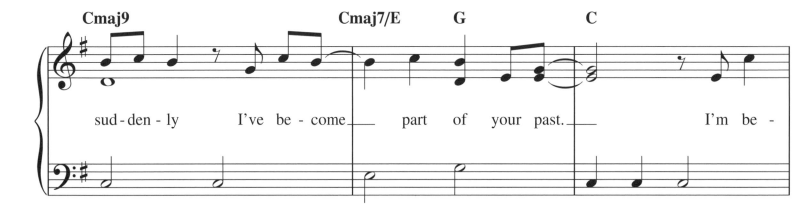

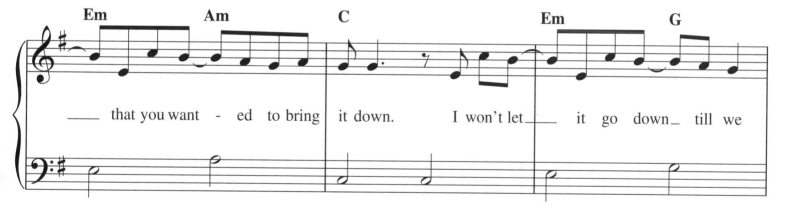

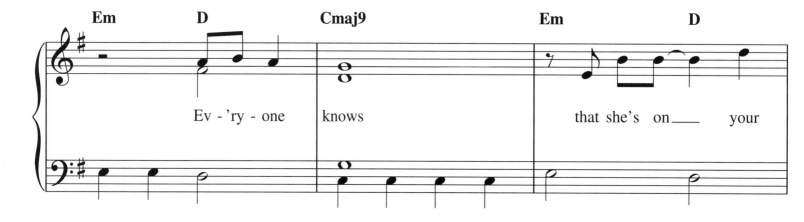

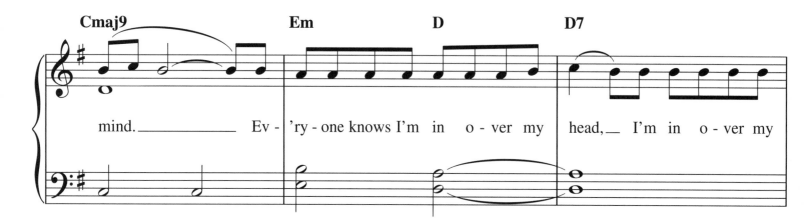

13

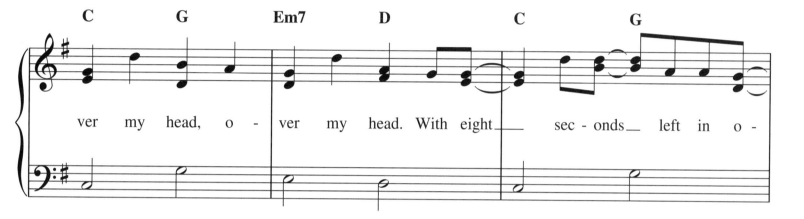

HOW TO SAVE A LIFE

Words and Music by JOSEPH KING
and ISAAC SLADE

Moderately

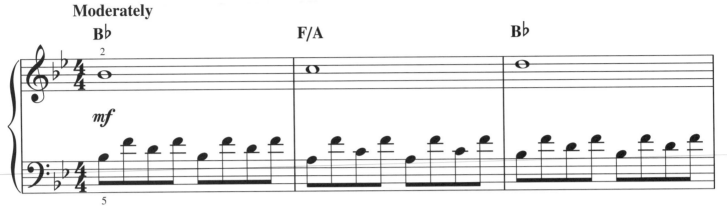

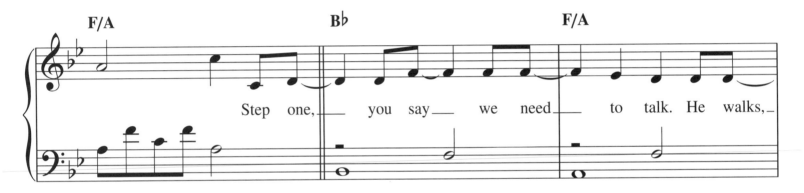

Step one, ___ you say ___ we need ___ to talk. He walks, ___

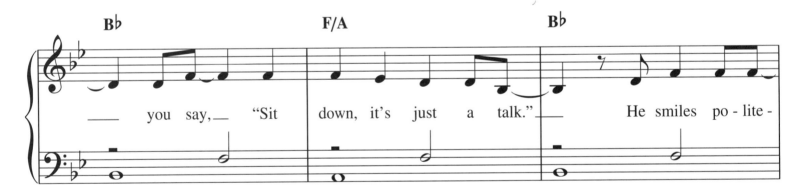

___ you say, ___ "Sit down, it's just a talk." ___ He smiles po - lite -

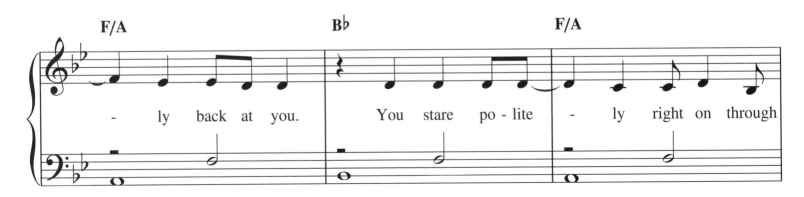

- ly back at you. You stare po - lite - ly right on through

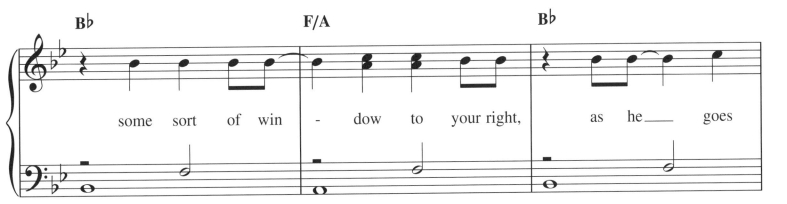

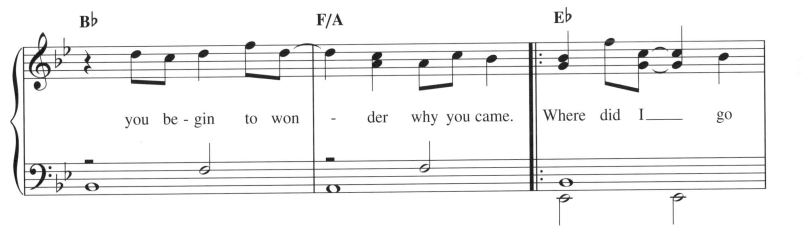

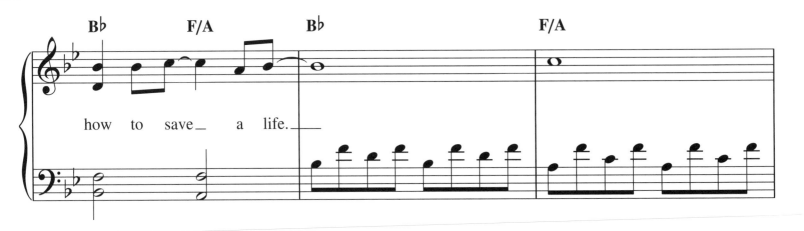

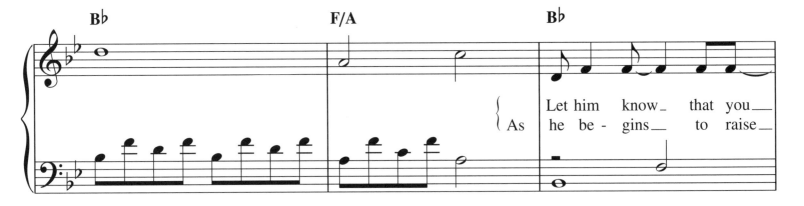

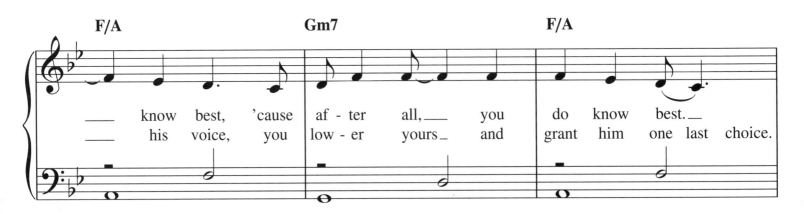

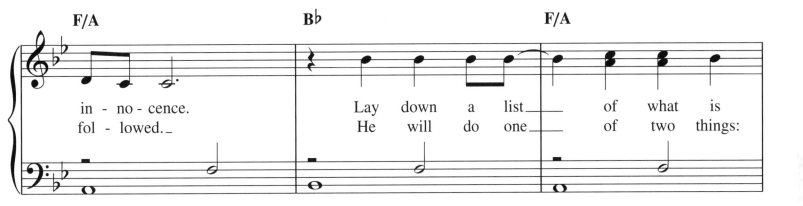

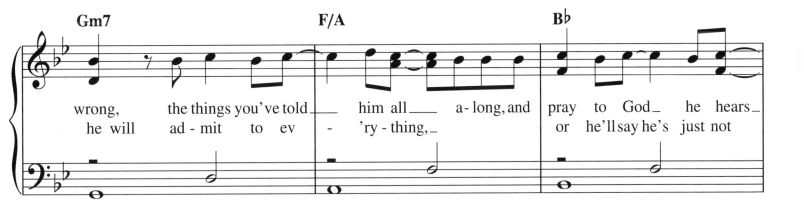

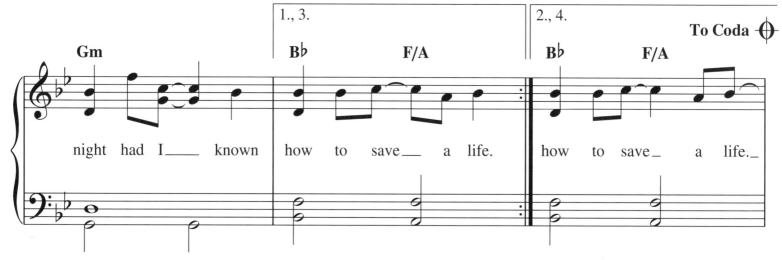

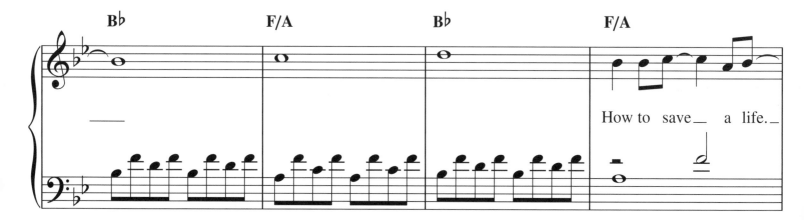

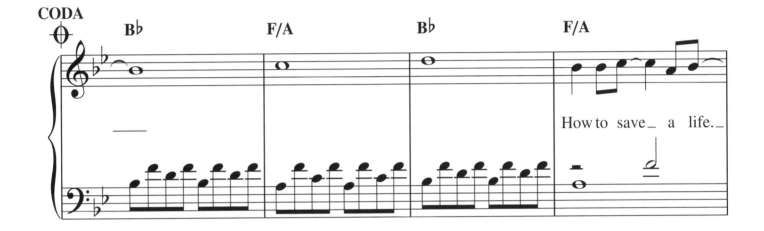

ALL AT ONCE

Words and Music by JOSEPH KING,
ISAAC SLADE and AARON JOHNSON

find a bet - ter one com - pared to her____

you, with - out____ a doubt, much long - er for____

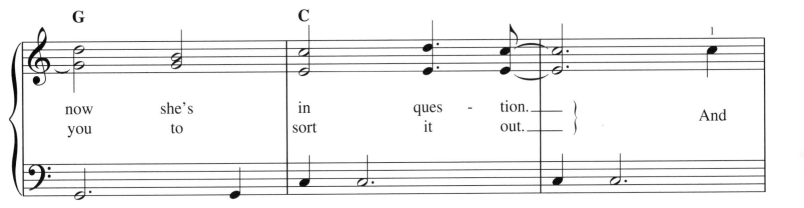

now she's in ques - tion.____ }

you to sort it out.____

And

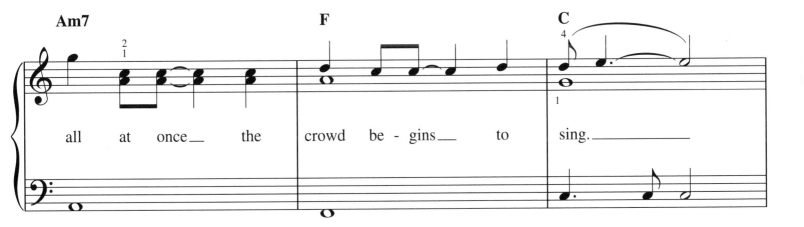

all at once____ the crowd be - gins____ to sing._____

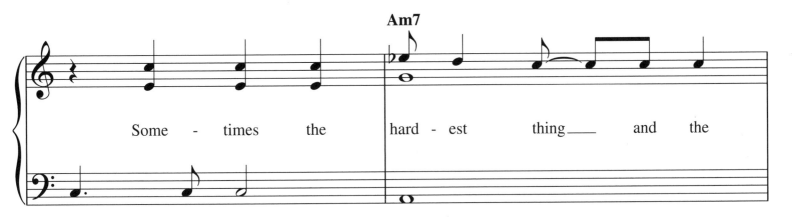

Some - times the hard - est thing____ and the

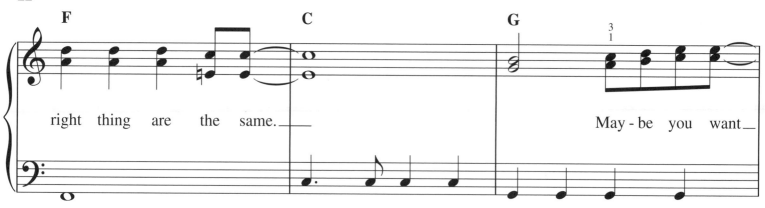

right thing are the same.＿ May - be you want＿

＿ her, may - be you need＿ her. May - be you start - ed to ＿ com -

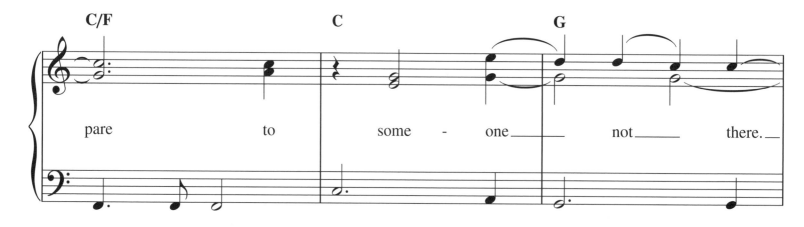

pare to some - one ＿ not ＿ there.

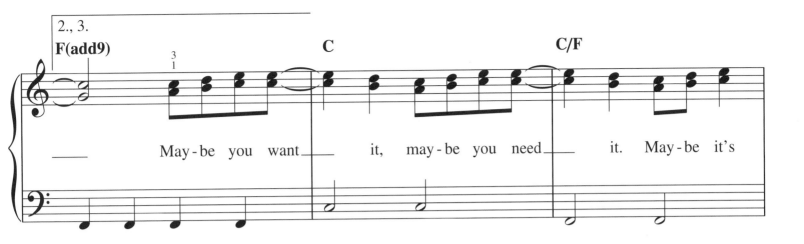

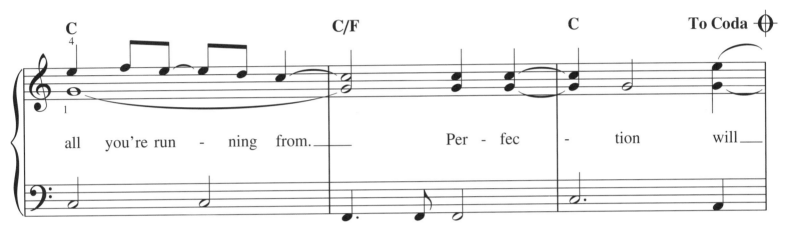

24

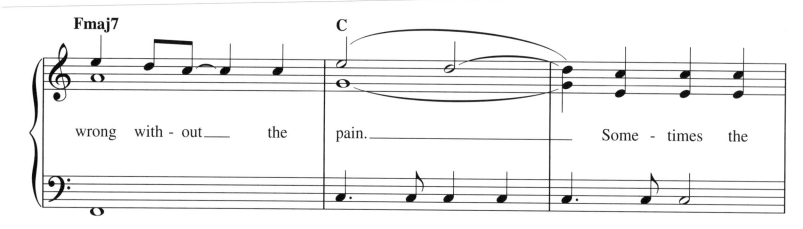

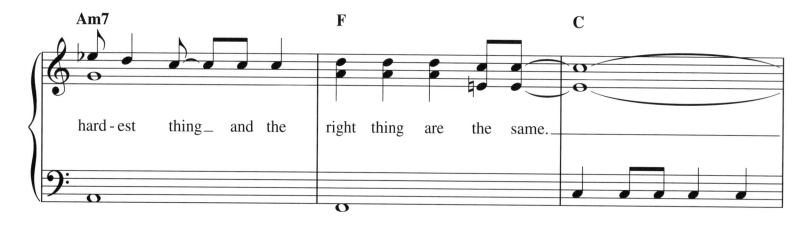

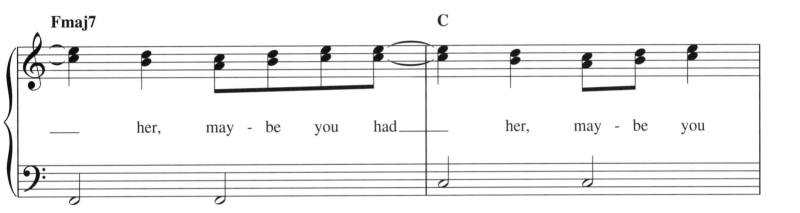

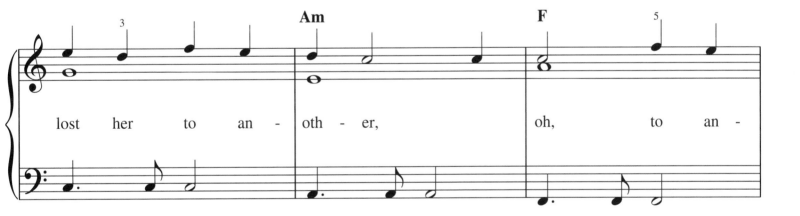

FALL AWAY

Words and Music by JOSEPH KING
and ISAAC SLADE

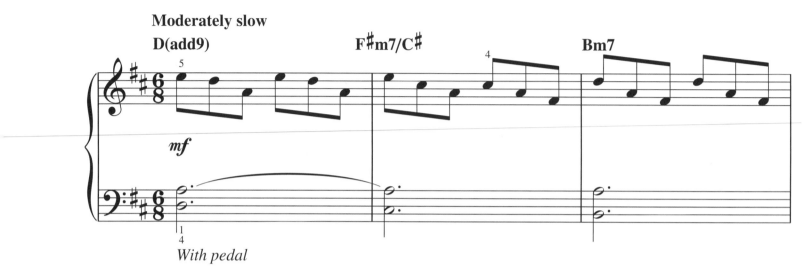

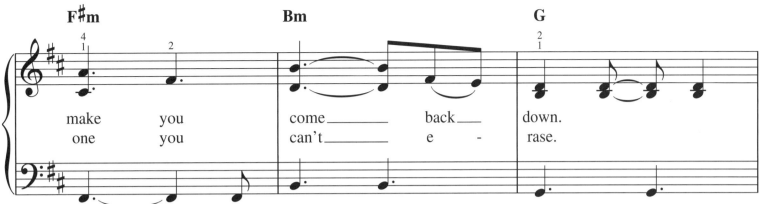

make   you   come_____ back____ down.
one   you   can't_____ e - rase.

      You made up your   mind_____   so   to leave it all be -
You   should have made it   right_____   you would - n't have to

hind.   Now you're   forced_____ to   fight_____ it
fight   to put a   smile_____ back   on_____ your

out._____   You_____ fall a - way_____ from your
face._____

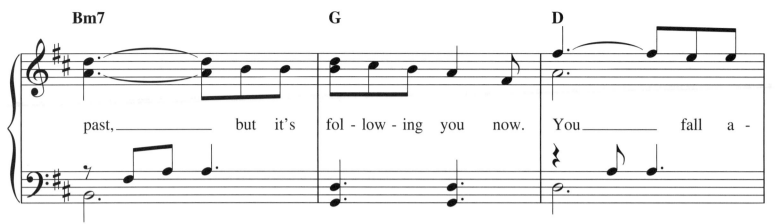

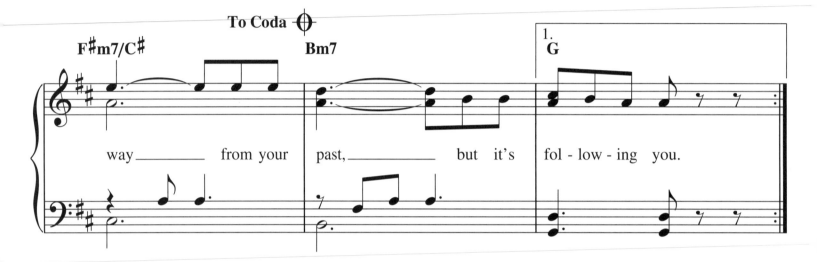

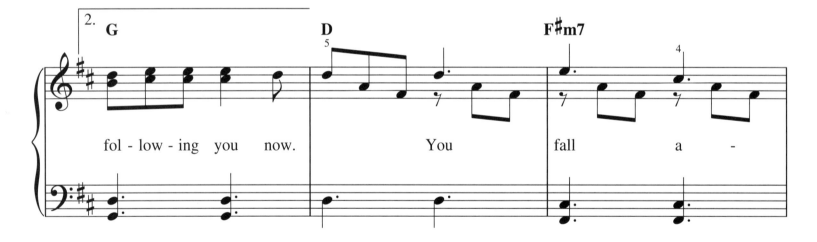

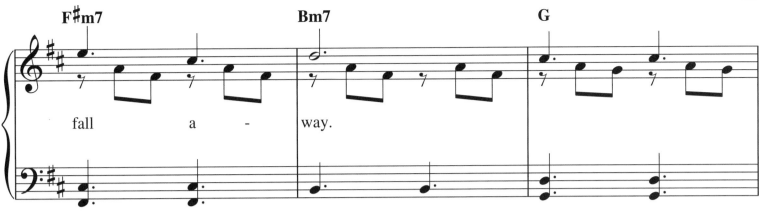

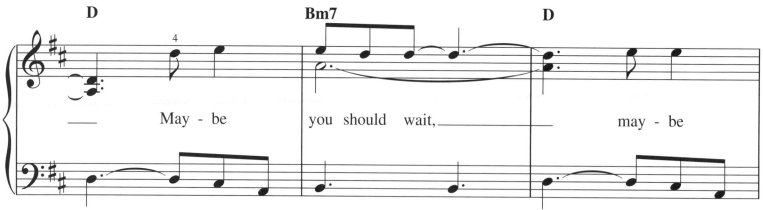

May - be you should wait,_____ may - be

you should____ run, but some - thing you've said_____

that can't be_____ un - done. And...

past,_____ but it's fol - low - ing you._____ You

fall   a - way._____   But   it's   fol - low - ing   you.____

____   You   fall   a -   way.

HEAVEN FORBID

Words and Music by JOSEPH KING
and ISAAC SLADE

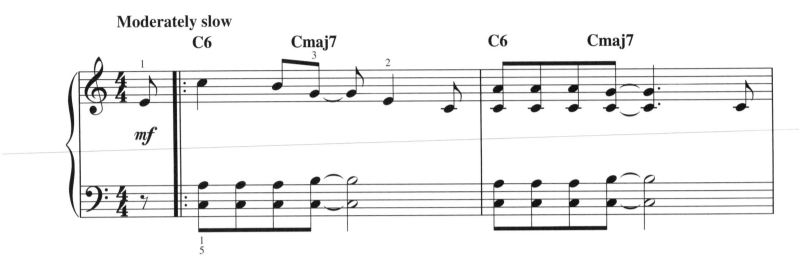

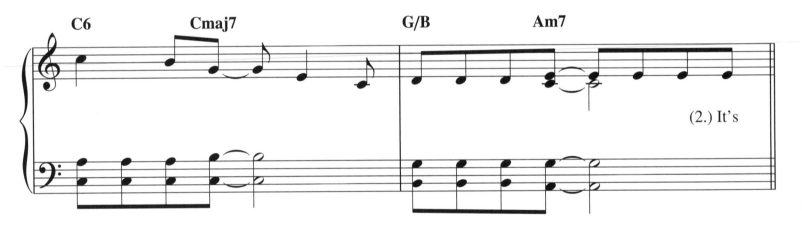

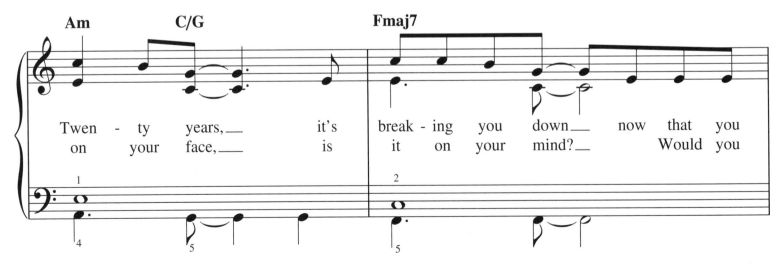

Twen - ty years,___ it's break - ing you down___ now that you
on your face,___ is it on your mind?___ Would you

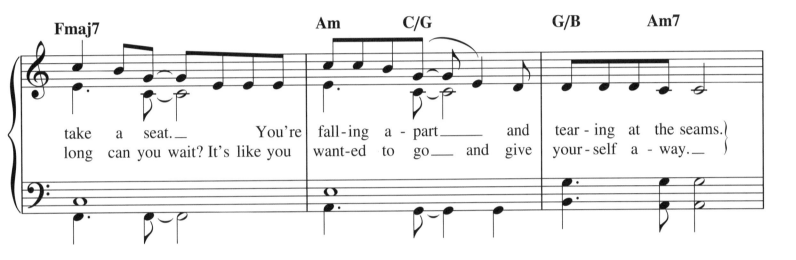

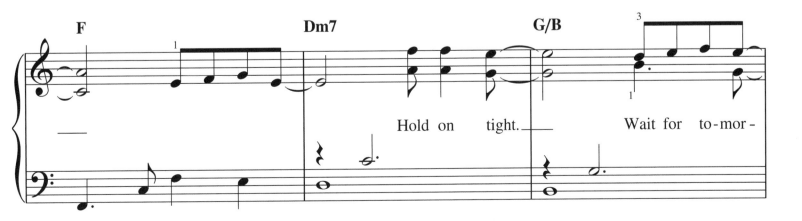

Wait for to-mor - row, you'll be al - right.

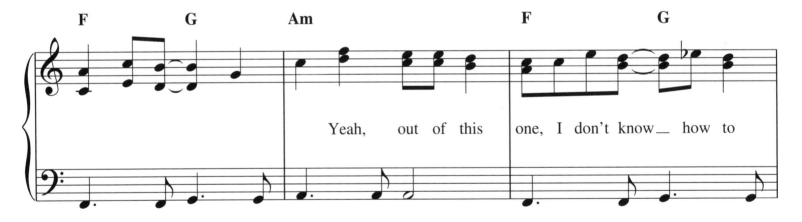

Yeah, out of this one, I don't know___ how to

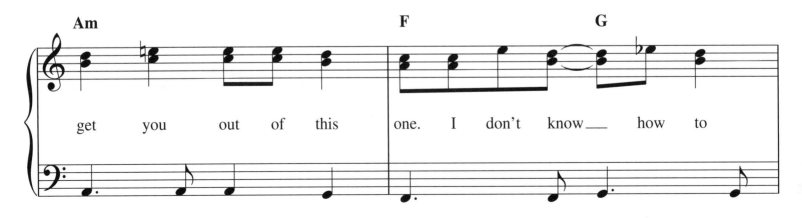

get you out of this one. I don't know___ how to

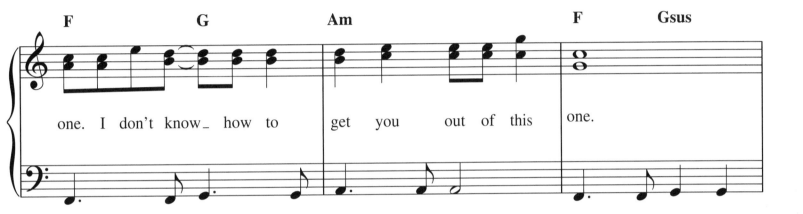

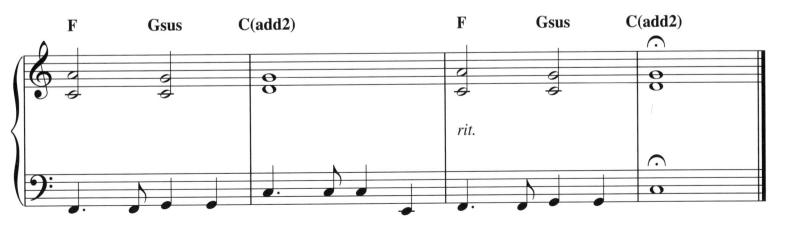

LOOK AFTER YOU

Words and Music by JOSEPH KING
and ISAAC SLADE

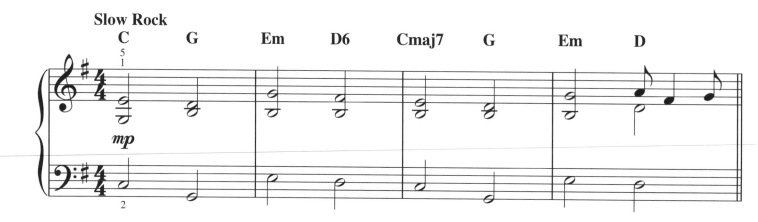

If I don't say this now, I will sure-ly break
There now, stead-y love, so few come and don't go.

as I'm leav-ing the one I want to take. For-
Will you, won't you be the one I'll al-ways know? When I'm

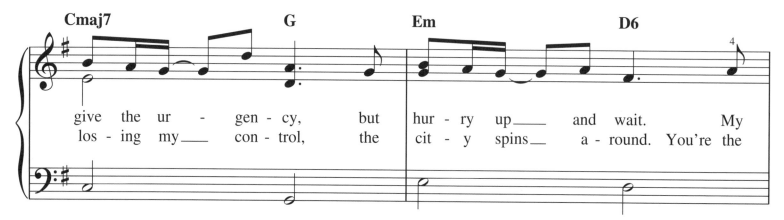

give the ur-gen-cy, but hur-ry up and wait. My
los-ing my con-trol, the cit-y spins a-round. You're the

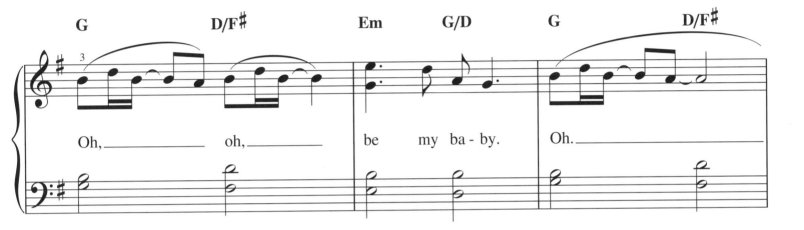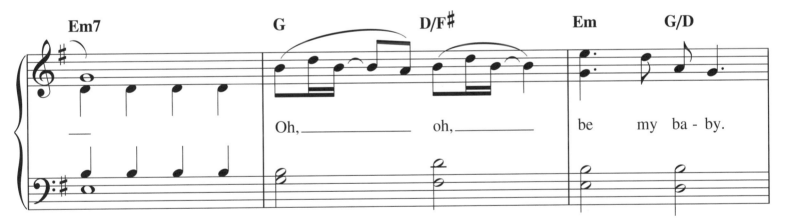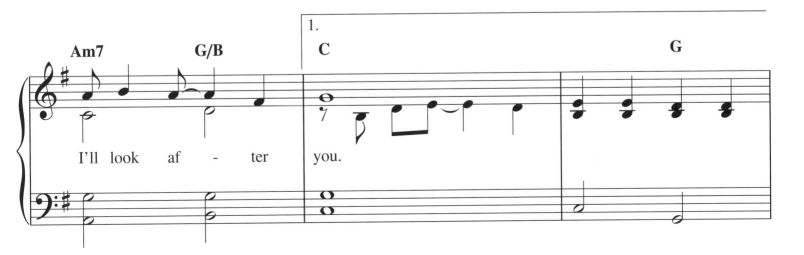

Em7   D | 2. C | Am7   D

you.   And   I'll look   af - ter

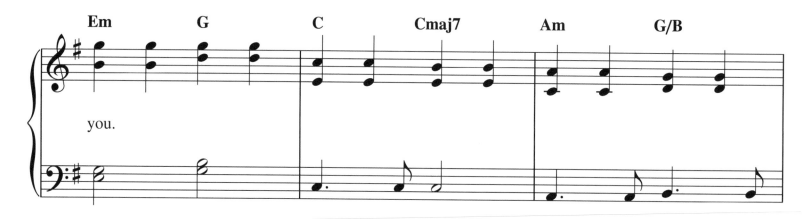

Em   G | C   Cmaj7 | Am   G/B

you.

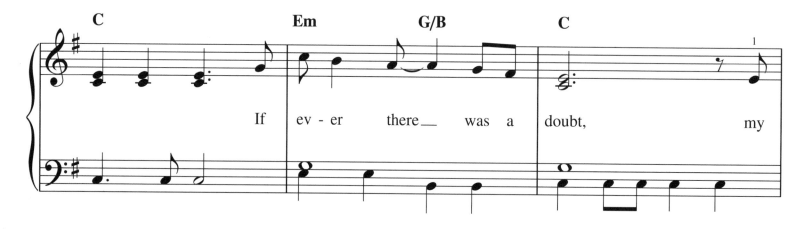

C | Em   G/B | C   1

If   ev - er   there__   was a   doubt,   my

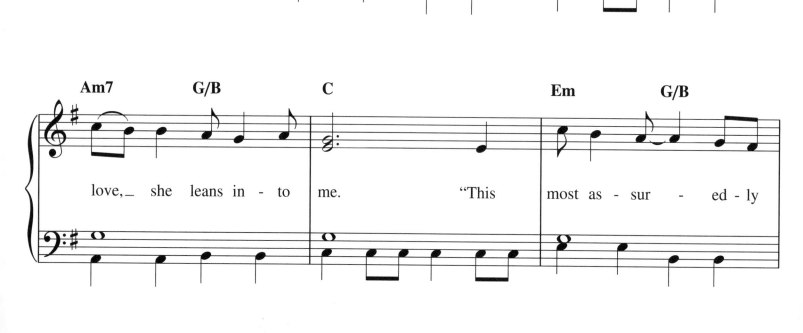

Am7   G/B | C | Em   G/B

love,__   she leans in - to   me.   "This   most as - sur - ed - ly

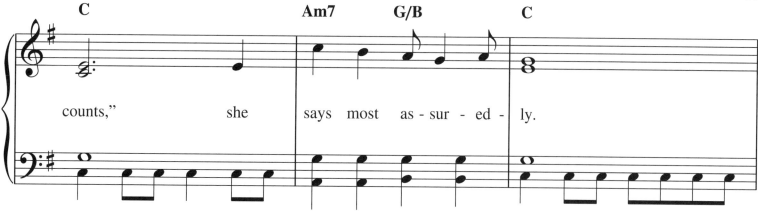

counts," she says most as - sur - ed - ly.

Oh,_____ oh,_____ be my ba - by. I'll look af - ter

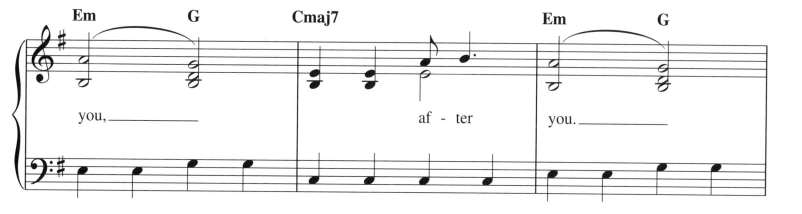

you,_____ af - ter you._____

Oh,_____ oh,_____ be my ba - by.

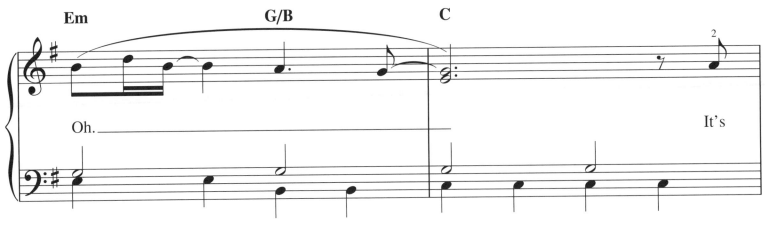

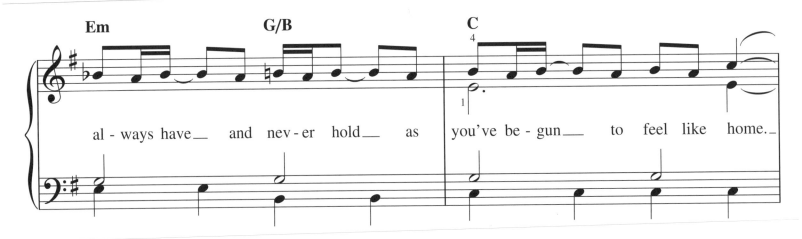

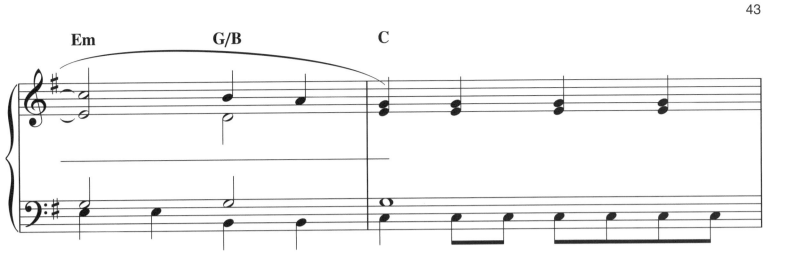

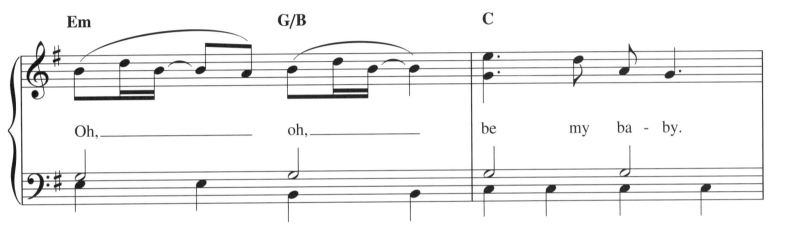

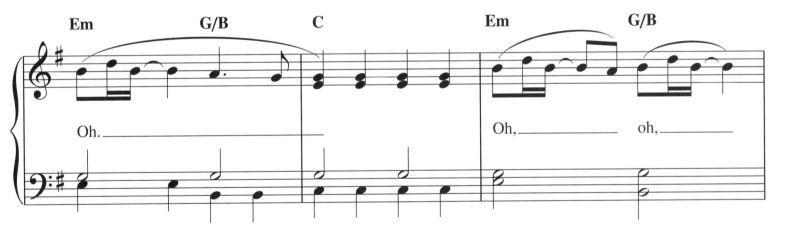

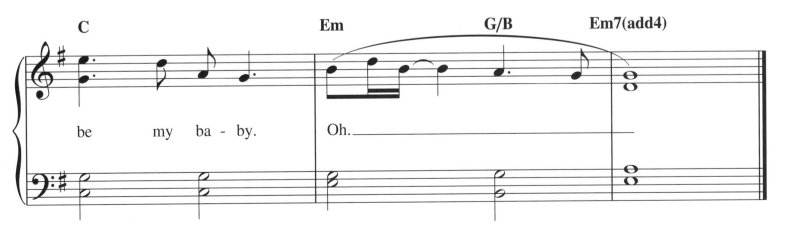

HUNDRED

Words and Music by ISAAC SLADE
and MONICA CONWAY

The how I can't_ re-call,_____ but I'm
hard, I must_ con-fess,_____ but I'm

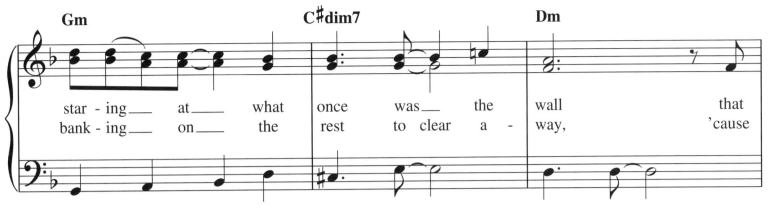

star - ing___ at___ what once was___ the wall that
bank - ing___ on___ the rest to clear a - way, 'cause

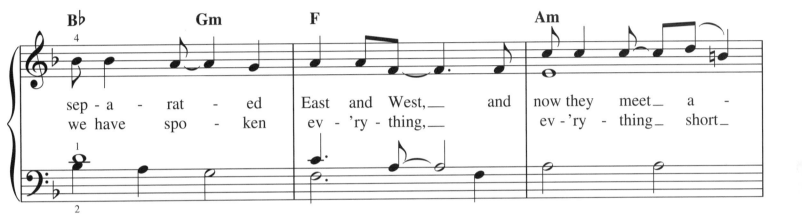

sep - a - rat - ed East and West,___ and now they meet a -
we have spo - ken ev - 'ry - thing,___ ev - 'ry - thing___ short___

midst the broad day - light. So, this is where you are___
of "I love___ you." You right___ where you are___

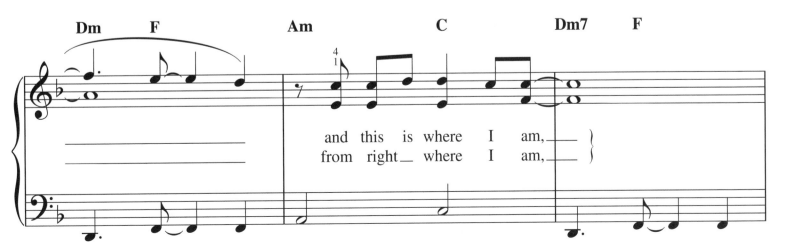

___ and this is where I am,___ }
___ from right___ where I am,___ }

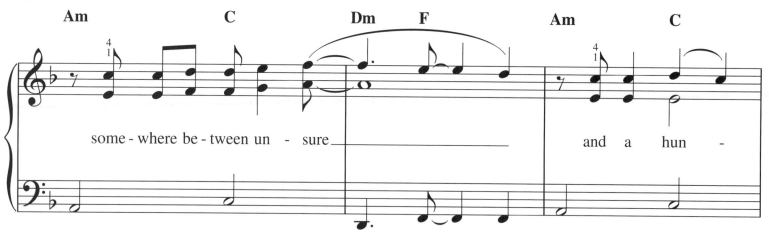

some - where be - tween un - sure _____ and a hun -

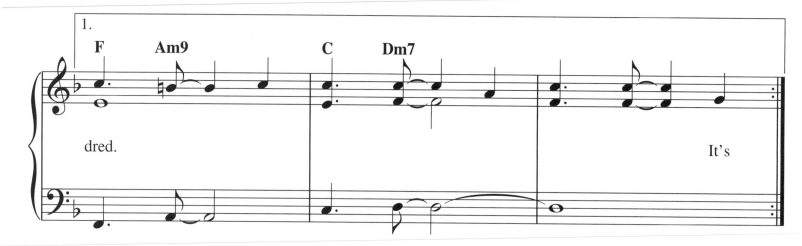

dred.   It's

dred.   Some - where be - tween un - sure _____

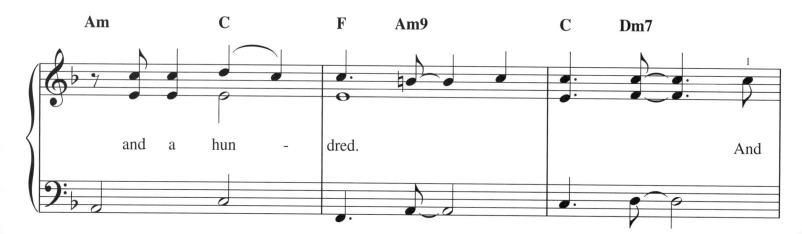

and a hun - dred.   And

who's _____ to say it's wrong,_ and who's _____ to

say that it's__ not__ right, where_____ we should be__ for

now?

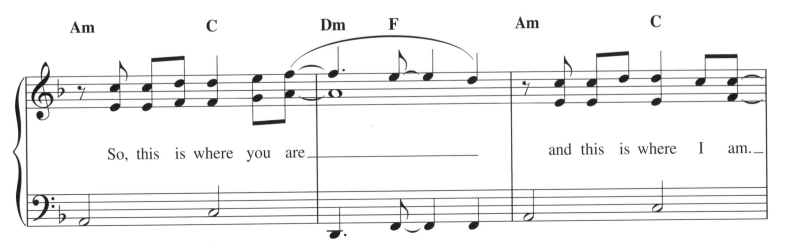

So, this is where you are _____ and this is where I am._

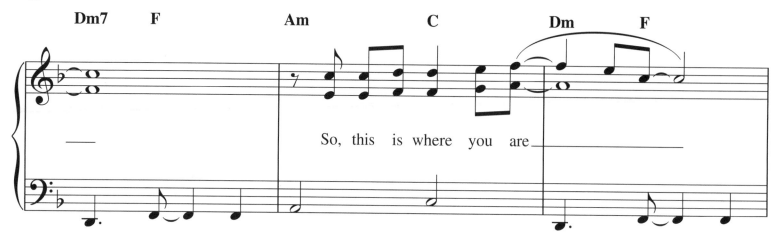

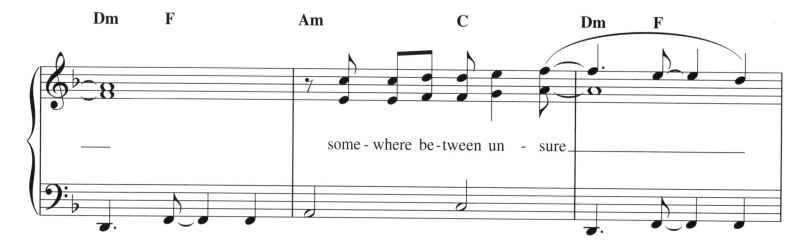

VIENNA

Words and Music by JOSEPH KING,
ISAAC SLADE and DANIEL BATTENHOUSE

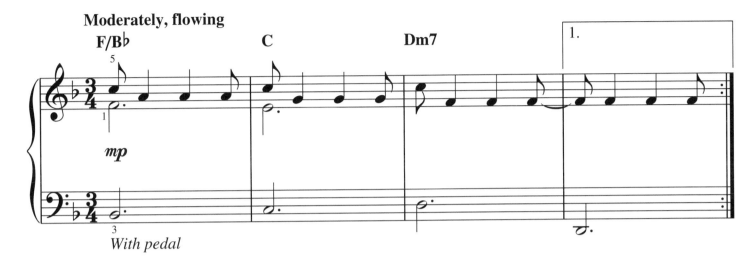

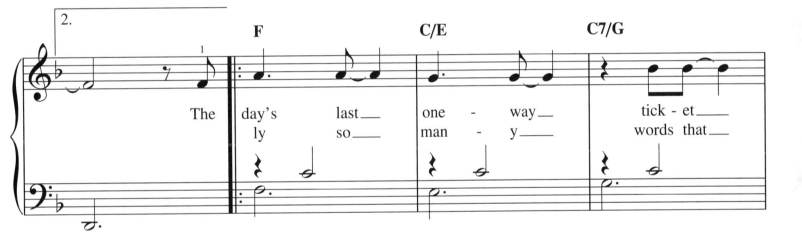

The day's last____ one - way____ tick - et____
ly so____ man - y____ words that____

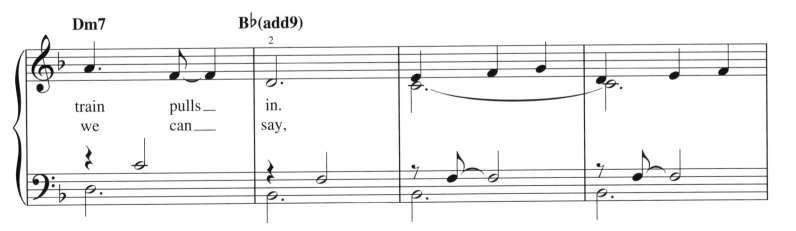

train pulls____ in.
we can____ say,

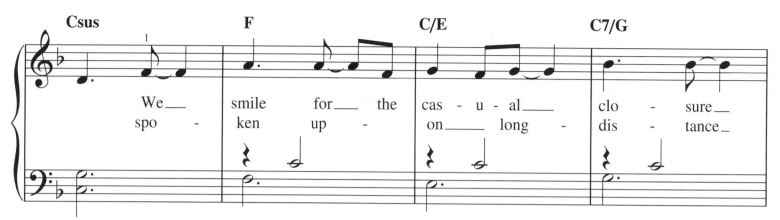

We___ smile for___ the cas - u - al___ clo - sure___
spo - ken up - on___ long - dis - tance___

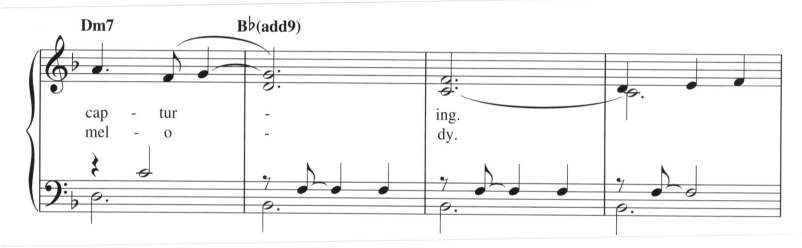

cap - tur - ing.
mel - o - dy.

There goes the down - pour,
This is my "hel - lo,"

here goes my "fare - thee well."
this is my good - ness.___

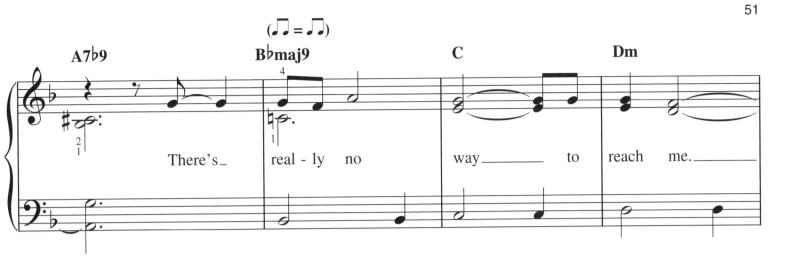

There's really no way to reach me.

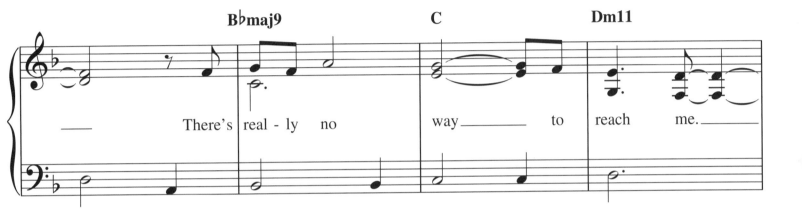

There's really no way to reach me.

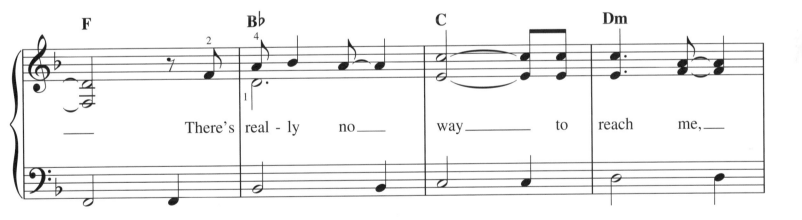

There's really no way to reach me,

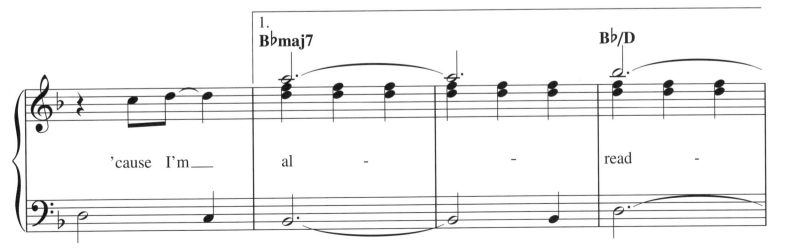

'cause I'm already read -

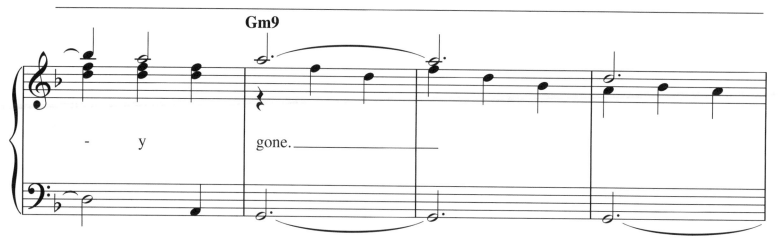

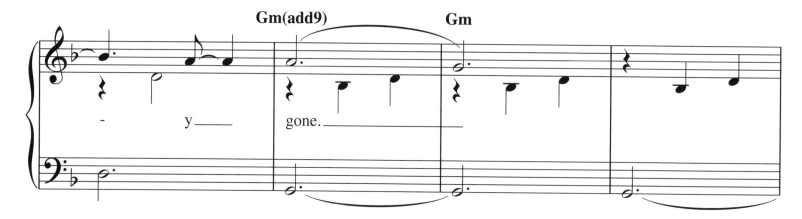

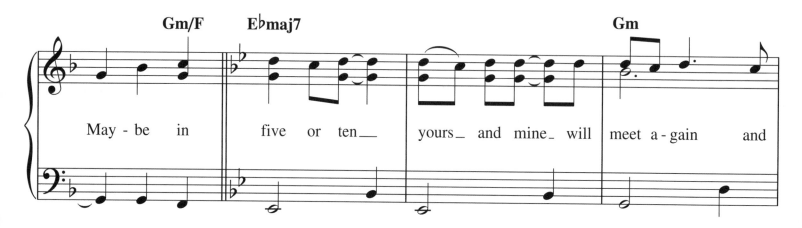

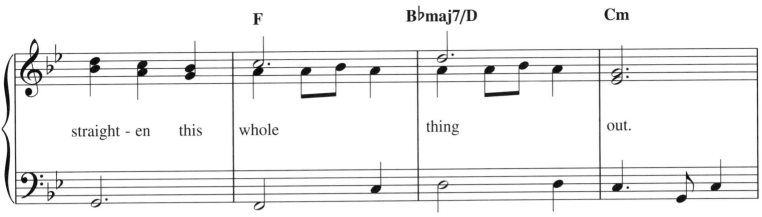

straight - en this whole thing out.

May - be then hon - es - ty___ need not be feared___ as___ a

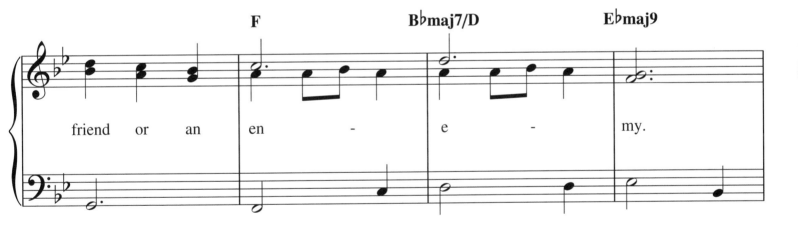

friend or an en - e - my.

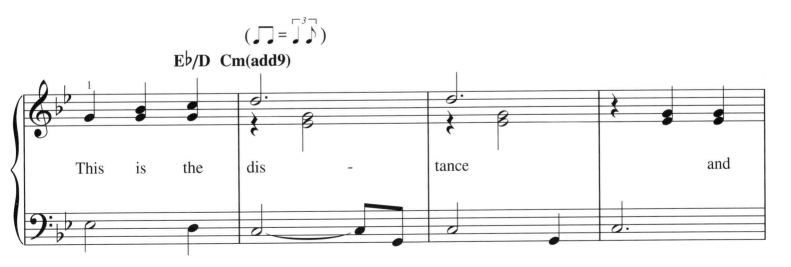

This is the dis - tance and

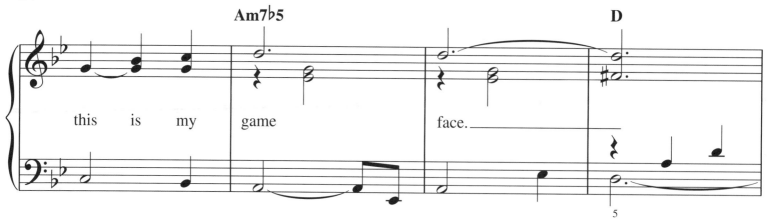

this is my game face._____

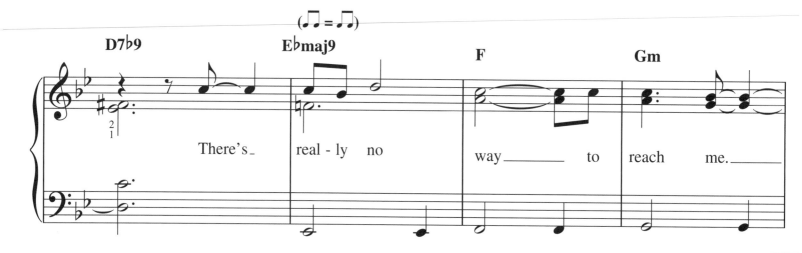

There's__ real - ly no way_____ to reach me.____

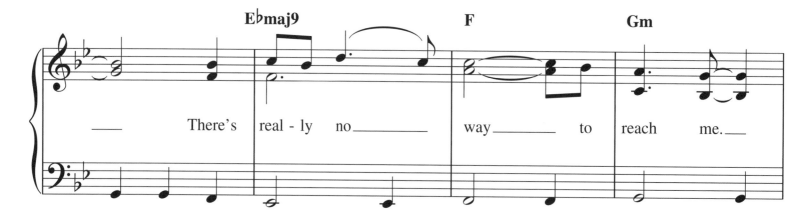

____ There's real - ly no_____ way_____ to reach me.____

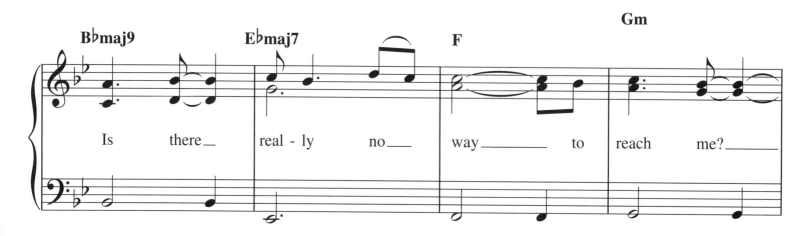

Is there__ real - ly no___ way_____ to reach me?_____

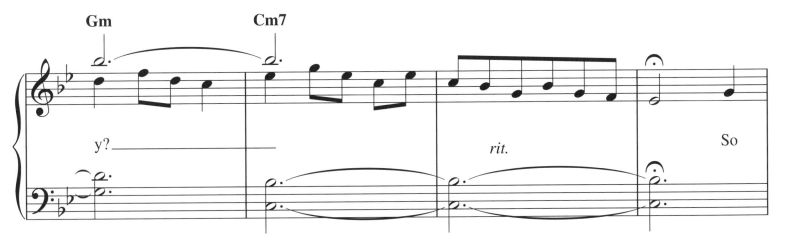

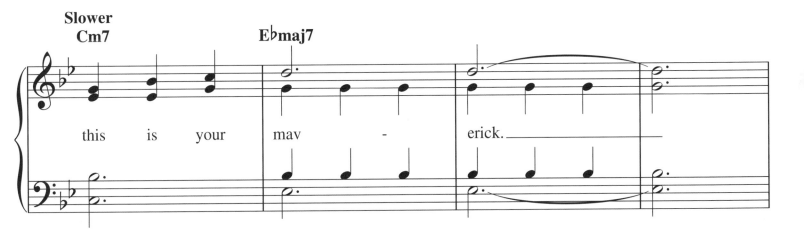

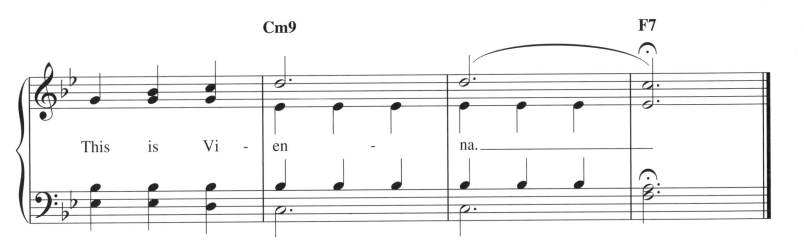

DEAD WRONG

Words and Music by JOSEPH KING,
ISAAC SLADE and MICHAEL FLYNN

Medium Rock

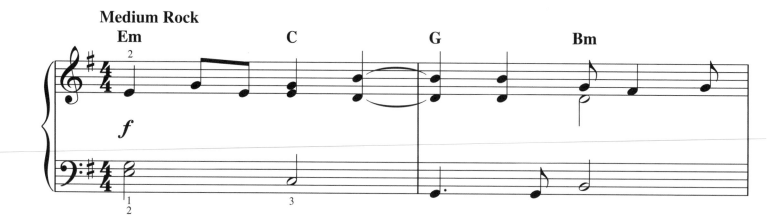

If on-ly I knew____ what I____ know,
I'm do-ing the best____ that I____ could,

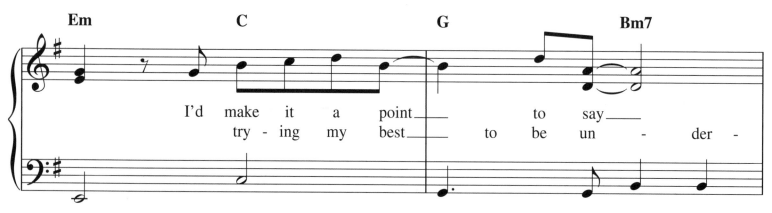

I'd make it a point____ to say____
try-ing my best____ to be un - der -

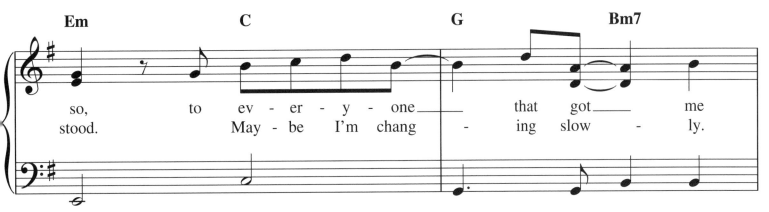

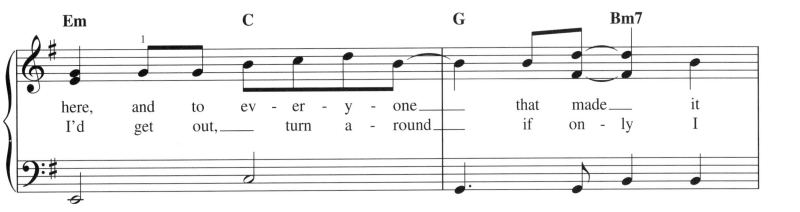

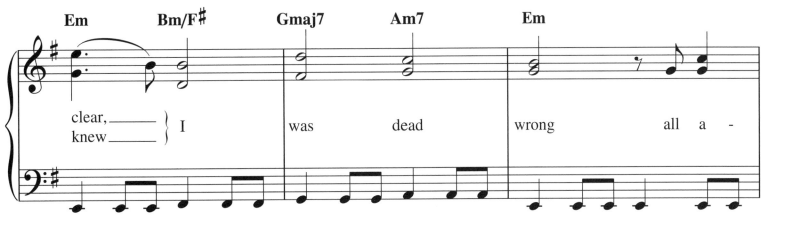

58

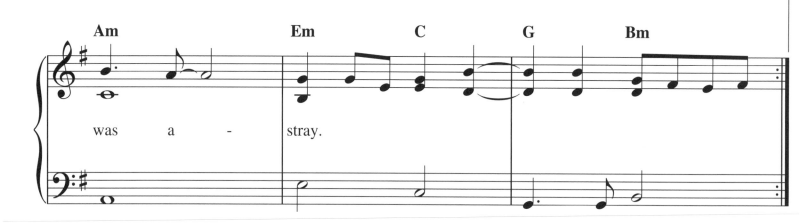

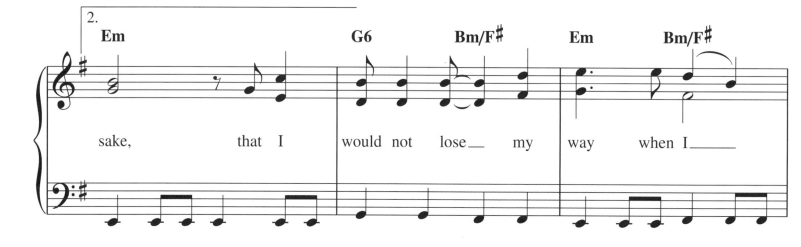

Mine is not a

new sto - ry. Mine is not a new sto - ry.

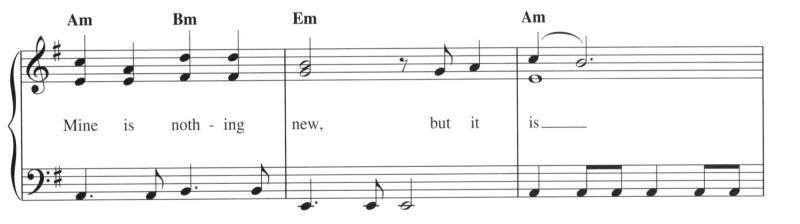

Mine is noth - ing new, but it is____

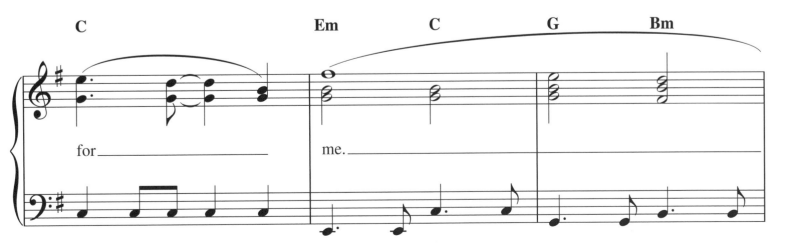

for _____ me. _____

And so _____ I

was dead wrong all a - long. _____ You

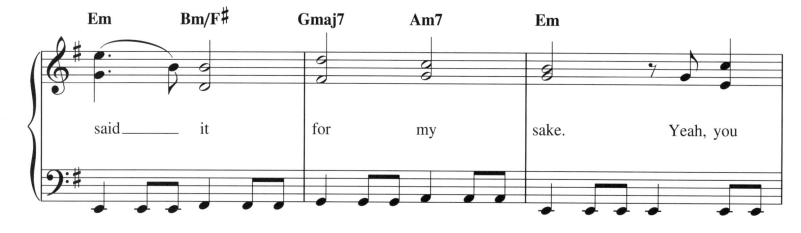

said _____ it for my sake. Yeah, you

thought I lost _____ my way when I _____

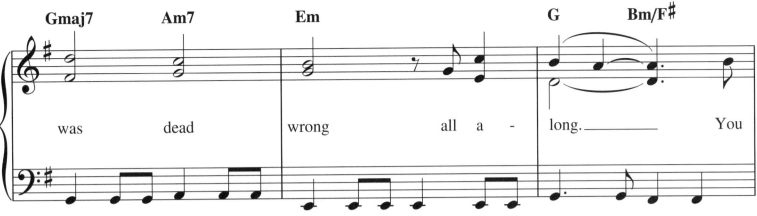

was   dead   wrong   all a -   long._____   You

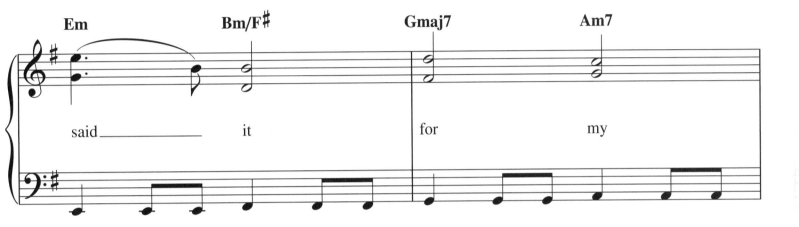

said_____   it   for   my

sake,   that I   would not lose__ my   way.   Did I

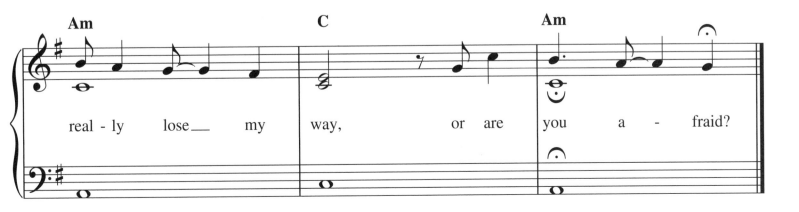

real - ly lose__ my   way,   or are   you a - fraid?

LITTLE HOUSE

Words and Music by JOSEPH KING
and ISAAC SLADE

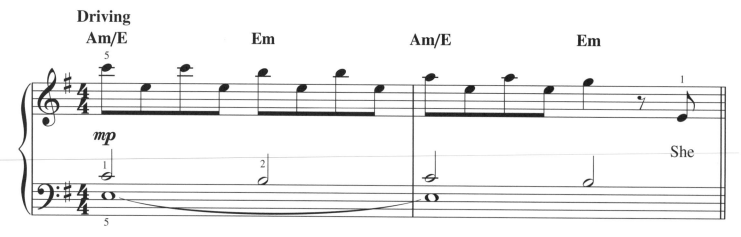

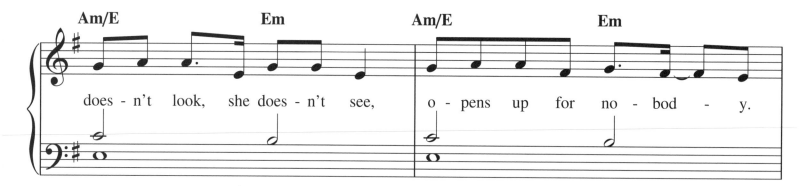

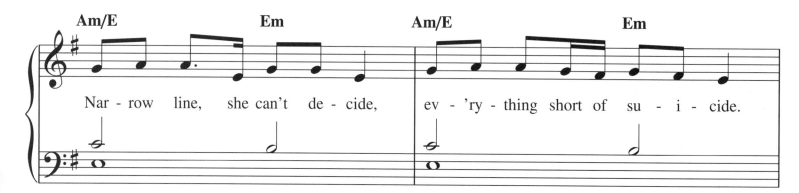

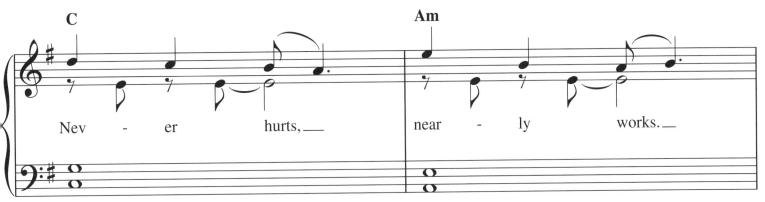

Nev - er hurts, ___ near - ly works. ___

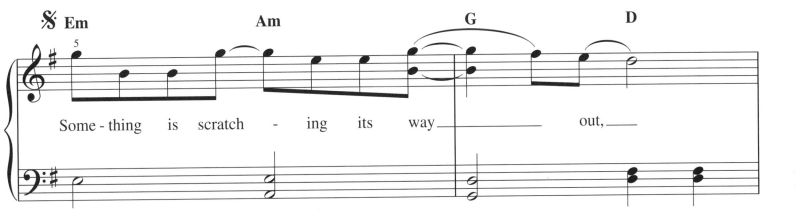

Some - thing is scratch - ing its way ___ out, ___

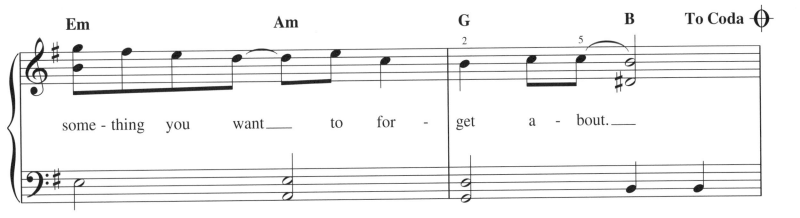

some - thing you want ___ to for - get a - bout. ___

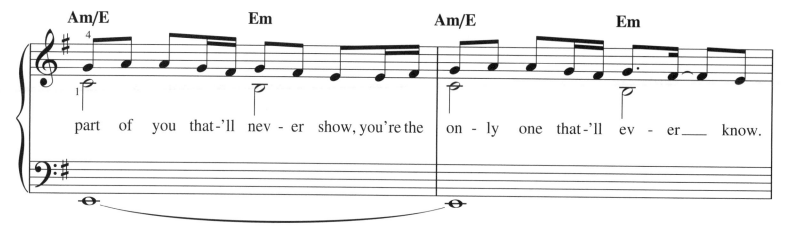

part of you that-'ll nev-er show, you're the on-ly one that-'ll ev-er___ know.

Take it back where it all be-gan. Take your time. Would you un-der-stand what it's

all a - bout,_____ what it's all a - bout?___

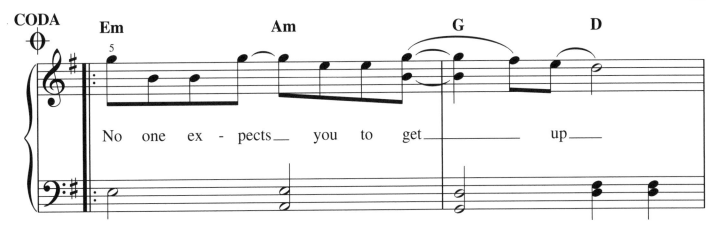

No one ex - pects__ you to get__ up__

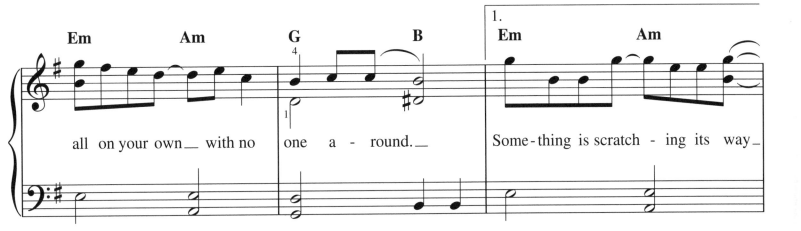

all on your own__ with no one a - round.__ Some-thing is scratch - ing its way__

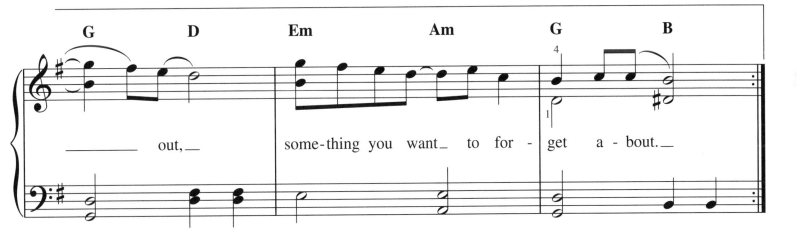

_____ out, __ some-thing you want__ to for - get a - bout.__

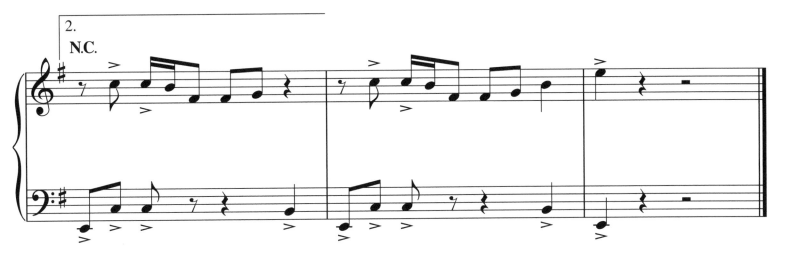

TRUST ME

Words and Music by JOSEPH KING
and ISAAC SLADE

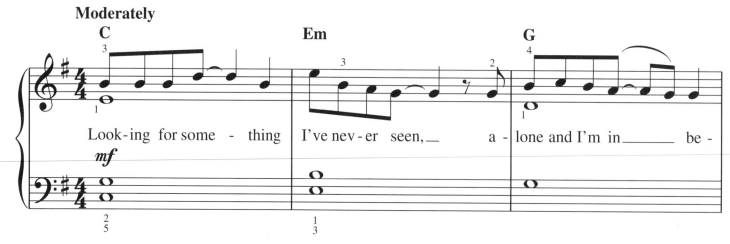

Look-ing for some - thing I've nev-er seen,__ a - lone and I'm in_____ be -

tween. The place that I'm from__ and the place that I'm in,___ a

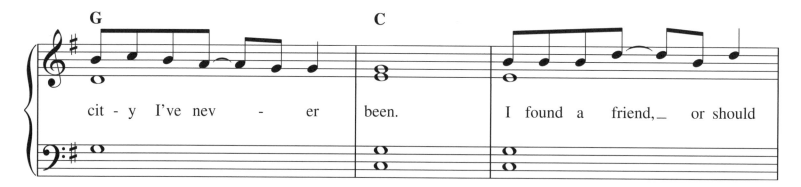

cit - y I've nev - - er been. I found a friend,__ or should

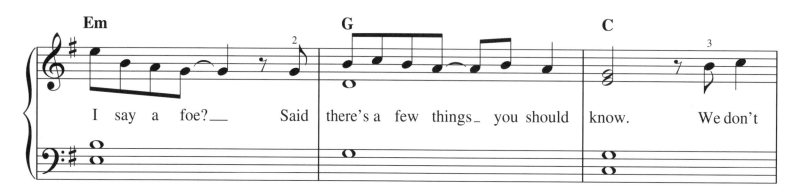

I say a foe?__ Said there's a few things_ you should know. We don't

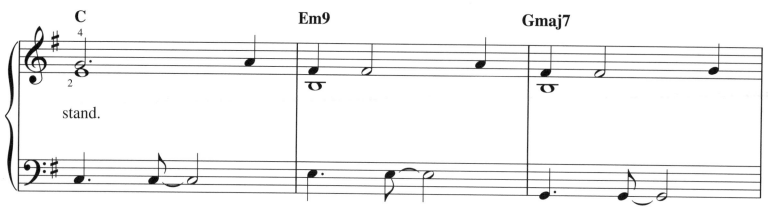

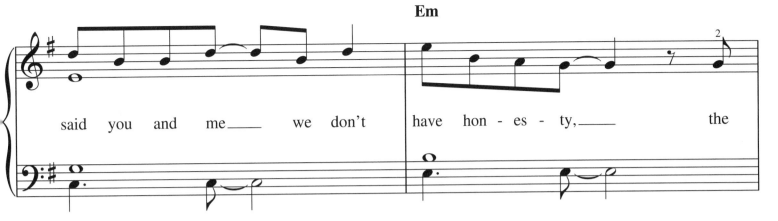

said you and me ___ we don't have hon - es - ty, ___ the

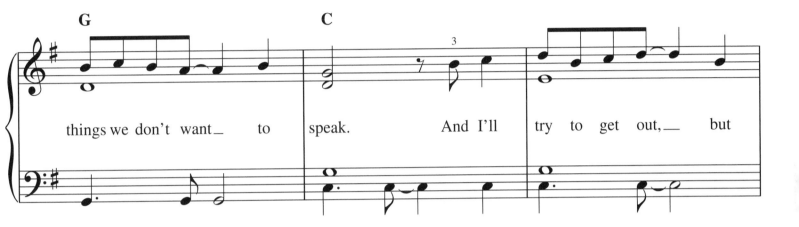

things we don't want ___ to speak. And I'll try to get out, ___ but

I nev - er will. ___ Traf - fic is per - fect - ly still.

stand. And then ___ a -

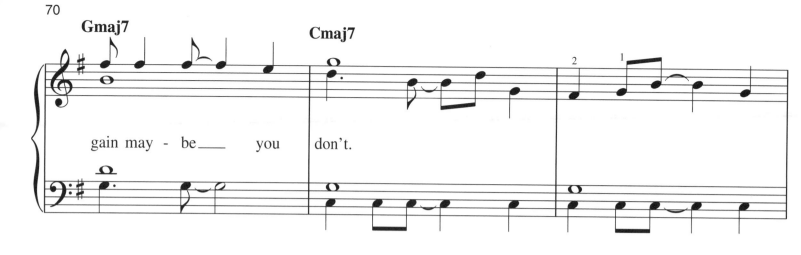

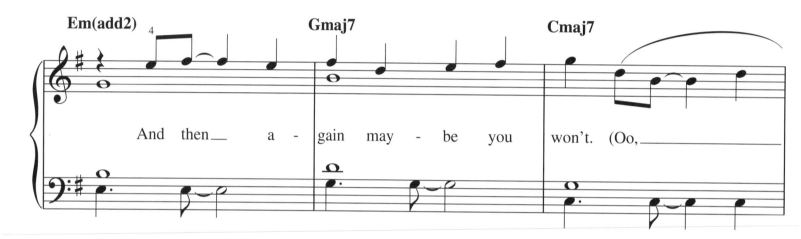

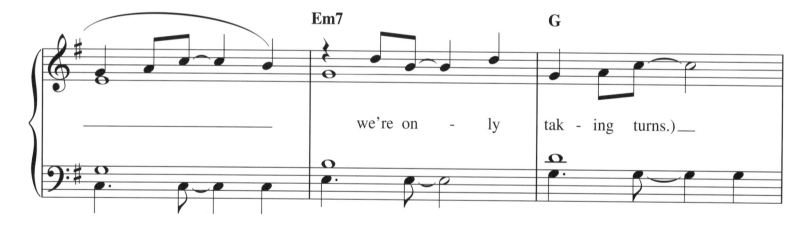

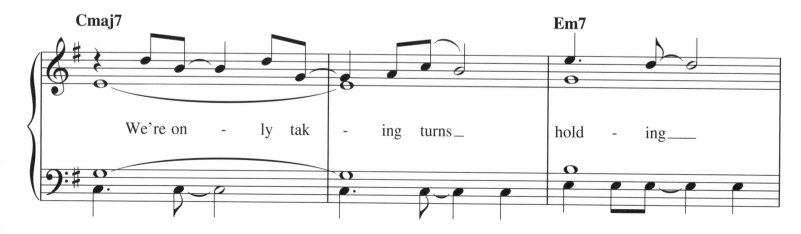

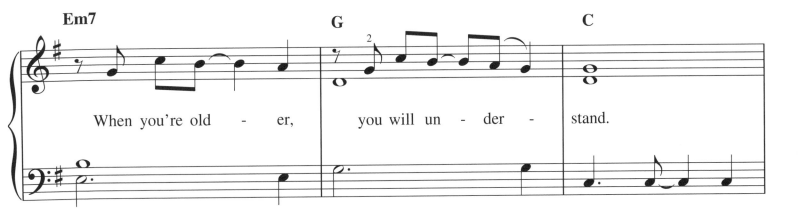